The JoyFull Journey

Lisa Saunders

Copyright © 2016 Lisa Saunders

All rights reserved. No part of this book may be reproduced or transmitted in any form or by any means, electronically or mechanically, including photocopying, recording, or by an information storage and retrieval system without permission in writing from the author of this book.

Unless otherwise indicated, scripture quotations are from the New American Standard Bible - Copyright © 1960, 1962, 1963, 1968, 1971, 1972, 1973, 1975, 1977, 1995 by The Lockman Foundation.

ISBN: 978-0692751466

Published by:

Lisa Saunders

www.lisa-saunders.com

Edited by:

Sharlyne C. Thomas

Spirit of Excellence Writing and Editing Services, LLC

www.TakeUpThySword.com

Acknowledgements

Thank you, God my Creator and King, for this amazing journey. You're everything to me.

Thank you, Anthony Saunders, my husband and forever love, for covering me and being the wind that carries me.

Thank you to all of my wonderful children. You inspire me to leave a legacy you can be proud of.

Thank you to my family for being my biggest cheerleaders and always believing in me. Whether by blood or not, you are me and I am you.

Thank you to those who have shepherded me along the way. I would not be standing in THIS place if it wasn't for you.

Thank you to my friends, ride-or-dies, sistahs and brothas in the Lord, for supporting this project. You believing that God has a WORD in me keeps my fire lit.

A special thank you to the woman who approached me one day and said, "You should be writing something. How about a devotional? If you write it, I'll read it." Marcy Bradley, this is for you.

The JoyFull Journey

"These things I have spoken to you so that My joy may be in you, and that your joy may be made full."

John 15:11

A Note from the Author

Beloved of Christ,

Welcome to your JoyFull Journey.

This devotional is designed to be a very personal, very intimate guide to a deeper relationship with Jesus Christ, our Great Shepherd. My desire was to simply share his heart – he is longing for a richer experience with his people and time away from all noise is critical to us being able to hear his voice above all.

One of the first things you will notice is that this devotional is written in HIS voice. This was intentional. It's one thing to have a friend, neighbor or even a parent call your name. It is quite another when Father God calls you himself.

As I said, this a deeply personal journey. It requires an honest assessment of where you are now in your relationship with Christ. You may discover that you'll need to pace yourself as you work through the devotional. You'll find areas where you'll need to "camp" for a while with your Shepherd. That is just fine! No one has a stopwatch on you. You can take as much time as you need so that you fully engage in what the Lord is saying. There are no extra points for brevity in your responses. If the space allowed to write down your thoughts isn't sufficient, grab an extra notebook and keep writing. The more authentic you are, the more revelation you'll receive.

Finally, I want to say TRUST your Shepherd as you go on this magnificent journey with him. Remember, his desire is to infuse us with his great joy. He's got you.

I pray that you have a JoyFull Journey indeed.

In Him Always, Lisa Saunders - Author, The JoyFull Journey

The JoyFull Journey

Table of Contents

i.   *Come Away (The Beautiful Invitation)*

ii.   *The Secret Place (The Place of Revealing)*

iii.   *The Alabaster Box (The Place of Breaking)*

iv.   *Selah (The Place of Reflection)*

v.   *Still Waters (The Place of Peace)*

Come Away

(The Beautiful Invitation)

> "My beloved spoke and said to me
> 'Arise, my darling, my beautiful one,
> come with me.'"
>
> Song of Solomon 2:10, NIV

Such a beautiful invitation. Can you hear the sweetness in my voice? Will you come, my beloved? For today, I am calling you away from the noise and the cares that have weighed you down in this season. I call you now to rise from the place of uncertainty, disappointment and disillusionment. Abandon all and come on a JoyFull Journey with me.

I can feel your trepidation even now. I hear the questioning: "Where are we going?" I know you love and hate surprises all at the same time. You love the thrill and excitement of the unknown, but not knowing drives you nuts. But when I, your Beloved, beckon you, it's my hope that your heart would melt.

If you could see my face, you would see it is so radiant with love for you. Do you trust me? Do you trust this divine invitation? Even today, I draw you with my love. It's a large love, and I know it's hard for you to comprehend it. I made you and I know your limitations. You do not trust easily – even me. But if you could trust me, you'd discover that my love for you is more than you can fathom. While many have spoken of my love, and volumes have been written about it, none come close to fully articulating it. My Word says:

> "...So that Christ may dwell in your hearts through
> faith; and that you, being rooted and grounded in love, may
> be able to comprehend with all the saints what is the breadth
> and length and height and depth, and to know the love of

> *Christ which surpasses knowledge, that you may be filled up to all the fullness of God." (Ephesians 3:17-19)*

It's an abandoned faith in me that will allow you to get a glimpse of my love for you, a love that up until now you've never really seen.

Tell me...

How do you view my love for you? Write it here:

> "Like a lily among thorns is my darling
> among the young women."
>
> Song of Solomon 2:2, NIV

You, my fair one, are such a beautiful creature – set apart among all that surrounds you. You stand out. Do you realize that? There is so much that is ugly and dark in the world but wherever you are, my face is automatically drawn there. Thorns may be surrounding you now. Yes, I've seen the situations and circumstances that have surrounded you in this season. The enemy of your soul would have you to believe that you are in a place where even I can't reach you. Let me assure you, my beloved, that this is not true. Doesn't my Word say that you cannot be snatched from my hand?

> "I give them eternal life, and they shall never perish; no one
> will snatch them out of my hand." (John 10:28, NIV)

Instead, even now, I hedge you in with my songs of deliverance.

> "You are my hiding place; You preserve me from trouble;
> You surround me with songs of deliverance."
> (Psalm 32:7)

Can you hear me singing over you? **I am your hiding place.** Come away with me and hear the new song that I am singing over your life even now. **I am your hiding place.** It's a beautiful melody. It's rich with notes full of my great love for you. Listen. Listen with your heart, my fair one.

Tell me...

What words do you hear when you think of me? Write them here:

> "Like an apple tree among the trees of the forest is my beloved among the young men. I delight to sit in his shade, and his fruit is sweet to my taste."
>
> Song of Solomon 2:3, NIV

Behold, I stand before you. Here I am. In the midst of all of the distractions that block your view, here I am. I am the lovely one. Come. Today, you can walk past all of the noise and sit in my presence. I promise you shade from the heat of the turmoil that's beating down on you right now. Come away with me and allow my words to enter not only your ears, but also your heart. My words will cancel out all of the bitterness that I can see growing in your heart right now. I don't count it against you that you've lost some of your faith in me. I know this season has been especially hard on you, but hear me today; I offer you respite.

Like an apple tree among the vast trees in a forest, I offer you refreshment right in the middle of the crowded place. I know that sometimes you feel utterly surrounded by the world, all of the obligations, appointments and commitments. As in a forest, it can be very easy to lose your way and get lost among the chaos. Each trial looks like the next. Each situation you must now overcome looks and feels like the last time. Soon you've strayed from the path that leads to a clearing, and you've become lost in all that surrounds you. Oh, my beloved, I offer you a way of escape. You don't have to feel this way. I have much to show you if you'll come away with me. I offer shade. I offer respite. I offer a cool place to lay down your troubled head. Enough time has been spent wandering in the forest of confusion. Can we depart from here? Together?

Here's my hand.

Tell me...

What stops you from coming with me? Write it here:

> "Listen! My beloved! Look! Here he comes, leaping across the mountains, bounding over the hills."
>
> Song of Solomon 2:8, NIV

Can you see me my fair one? Know that I will stop at nothing to come to you. There is no mountain or hill, no obstacle or hindrance that will keep me from getting to you. The walls that you've put up between us are no match for the tenacity of my great love for you. You see, I will scale any mountain just to see your face. I spare no effort to get to you.

You are not alone. No, my love, you are not abandoned. Didn't I say in my Word:

> *"I will not leave you as orphans; I will come to you."*
>
> *(John 14:18)*

The enemy of your soul would convince you that I've left you alone to fend for yourself. It's just not true. He doesn't want you to come with me. He doesn't want you to realize that the time we will spend together is very precious. Do you realize that it's in our time away together where I reveal the most intimate parts of who I am? It is here where our relationship grows. Oh, how I long to show you all that I am in your life if you would let me. I have so much to show you. There is purpose to your life, and I have the key that will open many of the doors into your next season that you only stare at right now. You're wondering how to break through, and the answer lies with me.

Oh, precious one, there is so much I want to tell you. Your future is so bright. If you would really behold my face, you would see the roadmap to your entire life etched there. I have a storehouse of treasure that's been set aside just for you. Come and sit with me awhile and allow me to reveal your glorious destiny. You know when Adam and I would walk together in the Garden, it was a most special time. I would tell him my purpose for creating him. He was the apple of my eye, just as you are – created in my image. He knew my voice and could hear me come to him through the rustle of the trees. We laughed together. I revealed the mysteries of my heart to him. All he had to do was ask. There are many facets of who I am that you have never experienced. I want you to become familiar with my character like Adam was. So familiar in fact that you would know if something was from me or just based on your knowledge of my character.

Tell me...

What are your thoughts on intimacy with me? Write them here:

My dear one, where is your joy? Do you even remember when you last experienced a deep sense of joy? Well here's good news: You'll find your joy in the fullness of my presence. Doesn't my Word say:

> *"You will show me the path of life;*
> *In Your presence is fullness of joy;*
> *At Your right hand are pleasures forevermore."*
>
> *(Psalm 16:11, NKJV)*

I want to restore your joy in this hour. Your smile fades from time to time. My heart aches when I see your countenance so downcast. I see the arrows that the enemy has shot at you. Come to me and let me restore your joy. I can just see us laughing among the lilies of the field. As beautiful as they are, they don't compare to you when your face is full of unabashed joy. I can give you back your laughter, the laughter you had as a child when the wonderment of the world around you made you chuckle with glee. I remember that laugh. I was there, dear child, always there. Joy was there and it can be with you again. Just come. Your joy will be full again.

> *"These things I have spoken to you so that My joy may be in*
> *you, and that your joy may be made full."*
>
> *(John 15:11)*

Conclusion: A wonderful invitation awaits you, my beloved. Will you come? My heart beckons to your heart. My hands, scarred by my sacrifice for you, reach out to you today. Let's get away from the place of stagnation and doubt. There's a place I've prepared for you and I to meet. I promise you, it will be a JoyFull Journey. Let's go, shall we?

Tell me...

What are your final thoughts about my Invitation? Write them here:

Closing prayer: Father God, thank you so much for loving me enough to invite me to go away with you. I know there is no better place on earth than to be in your presence. My steps may be feeble right now, but I ask you to strengthen me in the areas where I am weak. Help me to know that you desire only my good in this season of my life. I trust you Lord that this is a divine invitation. I am ready, Lord. Let's go. Amen.

Go Deeper

Set aside some time for fasting and prayer over the next week. Let your focus be on the following:

-Shutting out all voices that are contrary to the voice of your Shepherd.

-Identifying those things that keep you separated from entering into the presence of God (guilt, pride, unbelief, low self-esteem, fear, etc.), and asking the Holy Spirit for strategies to surpass those obstacles when the enemy surfaces them. GET A GAME PLAN!

The Secret Place

(The Place of Revealing)

> "He who dwells in the shelter of the Most High
> Will remain secure and rest in the shadow of the Almighty [whose power no enemy can withstand]."
>
> Psalm 91:1, AMP

My beloved, I bring you now to the Secret Place. I would have you to dwell here for a while. It is here that I will reveal my heart to you in this hour; and yes, I have much revelation to show you, my dear one.

Remember in my Invitation, I told you that I wanted to share my heart with you. We have much to accomplish in this season, you and I together. My child, we are in covenant partnership. There is nothing hidden that I do not desire to reveal to you at the proper time. In my Word I promised:

> *"Call to Me, and I will answer you, and show you great and mighty things,*
> *which you do not know."*
>
> (Jeremiah 33:3, NKJV)

You only have to look up and you'll see me.

There are secrets in my heart that I have prepared to reveal to you in this season of your life. They are a mystery to you now, but I know them fully. I hear the questions that are on your mind: Where? When? What? How? I know that nagging feeling you have that there is more to the story of your life. Oh, yes, there is — much more than you can imagine. There are keys I have reserved for you to unlock doors in both the heavenly and the earthly realms. The keys are hidden in my Word and are manifested to you as whispers in the Secret Place. These keys unlock the doors to your purpose.

Dear one, I know the enemy has worked against you non-stop to keep you from the Secret Place. He does NOT want you to know what I know. He has attacked your ability to hear me clearly. I know that even now, as you strain to hear me, you sense interference and opposing chatter. That is of the enemy. You have even gotten down on yourself when you feel like you cannot hear me clearly. Today, I am releasing you from that condemnation. Know that your enemy has done this, but he will not be able to prevail the further you retreat into the Secret Place. Do you see why you must come to the Secret Place, beloved? If you abide there (allow this place to be your shelter and covering), the enemy cannot succeed in stopping your ears from receiving my words. His plans are thwarted under the shadow of my wings. You would choose well to come into the Secret Place.

Tell me...

What does the Secret Place mean to you? Write it here:

> "For in the time of trouble he shall hide me in his pavilion: in the secret of his tabernacle shall he hide me; he shall set me up upon a rock."
>
> Psalm 27:5, KJV

My beloved child, know that the Secret Place is a hiding place for you when the troubles of this world hem you in. I hide you so that you can see my face and hear my heart. Yes, the plans I have for you are revealed in my heartbeat. Lean close to my chest and feel your future. Every beat represents another realm of my glory. You are mine and I am yours. You may feel forsaken by the world, but I've got you in the palm of my hand. I see all and I know all, and I won't stop pursuing you until you walk purposefully in all that is yours.

Do not let the trouble of this world intimidate you from pursuing me. I know that many present you with a different path to knowing the plan for your life, but those are bits and pieces of a larger, more beautiful mosaic that they do not fully know. Only I know and have every piece. These counterfeit plans are sent to confuse you. They take you away from the place that is your destiny. My love, do not settle in the counterfeit place.

I say in my Word that I will hide you in my tabernacle. Do you not know the significance of the tabernacle of the Lord? The tabernacle is my dwelling place. My glory is there, and all that I am is reflected in every aspect of its construction. I am in it and through it. It is here where I choose to hide you totally engulfed in me. The enemy cannot get to you here. It's my turf. It is a place of safety.

Even now, I reveal the schemes and plans of the enemy. His plan is to silence you and keep you from peace. He has tried to heap many troubles upon your heart, and he sends "worry" and "doubt" to torment you in the night seasons of your life. But he has no standing or authority in the Secret Place. He would not even dare to venture into my presence. You are safe here, my beloved.

Tell me...

What troubles you today? Write it here:

> "Now we see things imperfectly, like puzzling reflections in a mirror, but then we will see everything with perfect clarity. All that I know now is partial and incomplete, but then I will know everything completely, just as God now knows me completely."
>
> 1 Corinthians 13:12, NLT

My tabernacle is also a very intimate place, sacred and pure. My dear one, it is in this space where you are fully known. You stand before me naked and bare, yet you need not feel any shame. Nothing is hidden in the Secret Place, and that is o.k. I know this makes you uncomfortable, for you are thinking, "How can I in my present state come so boldly before a holy God?" Remember lovely one, that when I see you, I see you through the blood of my Son, Jesus Christ. You can come near to me because of his finished work (Hebrews 10:19-22). His blood says "access granted." You have no fear of rejection. I fully accept you just as you are. Can you see me with my arms open?

Even now, know that I cast an approving eye towards you. Do you know that you are beautiful to me? It's true. It is impossible for me to see you as anything other than beautiful because you bear the image of the Father. How remarkable is his work in you! You're not even fully aware of all that is inside of you right now at this very moment. You possess such marvelous gifts, and you overflow with purpose and treasure. This is what I desire to reveal to you in the Secret Place. Cherished one, would you let me envelope you in all that I am?

The time of REVEALING my heart to you is now and be assured that I will do it. Know that from now on, you will wear revelation like a coat. What is revealed to you in the Secret Place will protect you from the elements and the storms that rage all around you. Revelation will be to you like a bow and arrow. You will use it to hit the targets that I place in front of you. Can you hear "bullseye!" in the spirit? No assignment is lost even though you feel like time has been too far spent. Just know that I am the one who redeems time. You will not feel like you are behind much longer. Even now, I'm speaking "ACCELERATION" over you. The more you press into my presence and learn of my plan for your life, the more ground you will make up. A divine catch-up is on the horizon.

Tell me...

What assignments do you feel you have not completed in your life? Write them here:

Conclusion: We have much to talk about, my dear one. I hope that I've awakened your appetite to know more about the plans I have for you. The Secret Place where I will reveal my heart for you awaits your arrival. Glorious treasures await you there. I am waiting.

What are your final thoughts on the Secret Place (the Place of Revealing)? Write them here:

Closing prayer: Lord, while my heart has some trepidation about entering the Secret Place, I know that it's right for me to journey there with you. There is so much I don't know, yet you've promised to answer my every question. I know I can trust you. You love me with a love I can't even comprehend. Help me to know, Father, that there are no limits in you. I want desperately to enlarge my thinking and my vision. Today, I choose to grasp your hand and learn of the treasures you have for me. I am ready. Amen.

Go Deeper

Set aside some time for fasting and prayer over the next week. Let your focus be on the following:

-An open, ready and willing heart to accept all that the Lord will reveal to you in this time.

-Silencing the voice of the enemy who will come with confusion and challenge you on what you hear from your Father. Shut him up now!

The Alabaster Box

(The Place of Breaking)

> "And being in Bethany in the house of Simon the leper, as he sat at meat, there came a woman having an alabaster box of ointment of spikenard very precious; and she brake the box, and poured it on his head."
>
> Mark 14:3, KJV

My beloved one, now that you have allowed me to reveal my heart to you, I lead you to the Place of Breaking. Oh, how precious is this place in my eyes. I have wonders here to perform in your midst if you would but allow it. Many have run away from the Place of Breaking, thinking that the price to pay here is just too high; but know that for you, the Place of Breaking shall be a place of much praise. I promise.

I know your heart asks, "Shepherd, why must we go this way?" Let me assure you that it is for your good, dear child. Life has laden you with many scars and you carry far too much weight on your back. I see the unfinished plans and dreams. I see the heartache, the disappointment and even the cynicism that has crept into your heart. Oftentimes, I grasp for your hand and I find it closed because it is tightly holding onto something that you need not bring with you on our Joyfull Journey. It is why I lead you now through the Place of Breaking. I cannot allow you to faint under the weight of so many burdens. Have I not said:

> *"For my yoke is easy, and my burden is light."*
>
> (Matthew 11:30, KJV)

What you carry is heavy because it is not mine. You carry the baggage of seasons long since passed. Together, let's reconcile what "was" with the glorious "what will be."

Tell me...

What baggage can you honestly say you are carrying around right now? Write it here:

Let me talk to you about the woman with the alabaster box. This woman was quite special to me. You see, we had a bond of relationship that was forged in the fire of adversity, heartbreak, forgiveness and unconditional love. I accepted her as my very own, and she allowed herself to be drawn to me even without knowing fully who I really was. Yet her heart knew me even when her intellect did not. She trusted me. She opened her heart to me and into that heart, I poured the fullness of my wisdom and love. Know today that the same is true of our relationship, dear one. Oh, how I treasure my bond with you. It's been forged in the fire and rest assured that there is no surer bond. So will you, like this dear woman, push past the place where your intellect overrules your heart?

I understand, precious one, that going willingly to the Place of Breaking defies natural logic. "Why would anyone do that to themselves?" you ask. Let me tell you why: what comes from your breaking is an emptying that allows me to fill you with the precious oil of joy. The woman with the alabaster box knew in her spirit that I would be leaving soon, yet she joyfully relinquished all that was precious to her. Her "all" ministered to me in a way that no one else could.

Oh, that your heart would be like the woman with her alabaster box! You would know that this place is full of blessing. It was in this place that this dear woman broke open that which was precious to her and poured it all out before me. What a moment! The people around her misunderstood what it was she was doing. They ridiculed her. They mocked her. They misinterpreted her tears; those were not tears of sadness but tears of praise. They could not fully comprehend the extent of our love relationship but I, my love, completely understood. She allowed the breaking of what was precious to her because she knew it would be for my praise and glory. Do you trust me like this dear woman?

Tell me...

What do you think about the precious woman with the alabaster box? Write it here:

> "The sacrifices of God are a broken spirit; a broken and contrite heart, O God, you will not despise."
>
> Psalm 51:17, ESV

My beloved, don't you know that your breaking is worship to me? Your broken pieces sing to me, and the sound reaches my ears as a beautiful symphony. It is a melody that is precious and unique, every note and crescendo signifying a deeper trust in me. It's so sweet and wonderful. Come. See the beauty in your brokenness.

You feel as if you're standing among ruins, but what appears to you as broken dreams and shattered promises on the floor of despair are glorious pieces of a future hope to me. There is such a greatness and a freedom that lies just beyond the shell of what is your "now" place. My precious one, it breaks my heart to see that you've become so familiar with your pain; and yes, I know the temptation to not let go of that which is familiar. It's hard. My servants Abraham and Moses had to do it. Elijah and Elisha had to do it. The twelve that I chose to follow me had to do it. They were all called to step beyond the familiar place into the unfamiliar with only a promise from me that things would be better on the other side. But think about it, my beloved: In every one of those instances, my servants were able to realize their greater purpose in me. It is not easy but I assure you, it is worth it!

Today, I'm asking you to look at what's in your hands and see the potential that lies within them. Your great sacrifice shall surely be rewarded. Doesn't my Word say that anyone who leaves the things they treasure most to follow me will receive more from me in the end (Matthew 19:29)? It is a fair exchange, beloved. Trust me. And what are the things you're holding on to anyway? Of what value have they been? Has your life been better because you hold them so dear? The familiarity with brokenness in this world is so rampant that many would choose to hold onto the very things that crush them instead of surrendering them at my altar of sacrifice. They cannot see, or will not believe, that I offer so much more. But I pray this is not you, beloved. Will you trust me?

Tell me…

Can you think of some things that you may be holding on to that you find very difficult to let go of? Write them here:

> "Do not fear, for you will not be ashamed;
> Neither be disgraced, for you will not be put to shame..."
>
> Isaiah 54:4, NKJV

My precious one, as you consider this Place of Breaking, please be assured that your brokenness will not be a badge of shame. I will honor your supreme sacrifice. Yes, I've seen all the places where you've been broken where the enemy attacked you and broke not only your will, but your spirit. Your strength left you. Your courage left you. You forgot that my face is ever beholding your walls:

> "Can a woman forget her nursing child And have no compassion on the son of her womb? Even these may forget, but I will not forget you. Behold, I have inscribed you on the palms of My hands; Your walls are continually before Me."
>
> Isaiah 49:15-16

Oh, child, trust me and know that THIS breaking is far different. Where the enemy devised your broken places of the past to be chasms that he would occupy with depression, anxiety, hopelessness, drought, lack, doubt, unbelief and useless, I shall step into this Place of Breaking and fill it with peace, love and a renewed joy for your next season. What lies before you, my beloved one, is a season of exponential growth and prosperity.

So now you must dare to walk past the stares with no fear, take up your shame and come to me just like the woman with the alabaster box. She came to me. She took up her shame, walked past the whispers and stares, and came after me. I never saw her. Neither did I touch her. She touched me just like the dear woman who suffered bleeding and brokenness for twelve long years. Of all the people who touched me in that crowded space that day, it was her touch that grabbed my attention. Why? Because I KNEW someone had just made an urgent demand on my power. That dear woman didn't just TOUCH ME, she DREW FROM ME. At her moment of healing, her shame disappeared. Her faith in all that I am healed her completely. Will you be like this woman, dear one? Will you, too, take up your shame, bring it me and exchange it for the greatest healing you have ever known? I promise, you will not be disappointed. My Word says:

> *"I sought the LORD, and He answered me, And delivered me from all my fears. They looked to Him and were radiant, And their faces will never be ashamed."*
>
> *Psalm 34:4-5*

I've got you, my love.

> "O you afflicted one,
> Tossed with tempest, *and* not comforted,
> Behold, I will lay your stones with colorful gems,
> And lay your foundations with sapphires.
> I will make your pinnacles of rubies,
> Your gates of crystal,
> And all your walls of precious stones."
>
> Isaiah 54:11-12

My lovely one, if you could see yourself on the other side of the Place of Breaking, your natural mind would barely be able to comprehend what it would behold. Your heart would explode because like Joseph's coat of many colors, you would emerge from the Place of Breaking arrayed in the jewels of deliverance: Ruby (rare and precious), Sapphire (sprinkled with the gold that comes with affliction), Crystal (signifying abundance and transparency). Oh, how beautiful you will be! Can you imagine it? Your new colors will SHOUT to the world! Your cloak of heaviness will be gone, and you will dance in radiant, colorful joy!!

Do you remember a time when you were in a store trying on the perfect outfit? You tried it on and immediately you wanted to run out of the dressing room and let everyone see it. So you will be when you emerge in the beauty of your deliverance, arrayed in the splendor of a King who loves you. Get ready to dance, dear one. Get ready to dance!

Tell me...

What are your final thoughts on the alabaster box (the Place of Breaking)? Write them here:

Conclusion: Whew! I know that wasn't easy, dear one. Being broken never is. I know that. If there was any other way for me to remake you, I would have done it. I had to be sure that no vestiges remained of the past. A broken base poorly mended never regains its original form. That was my intention for you, that you would NEVER look like your past. Trust me. All is well.

Closing prayer: Lord Jesus, I willingly bring my alabaster box to your feet – for it is you only that I worship. Who in heaven do I have but you? I trust you to lovingly break me so that I will be whole again in and through your love. I realize today that I have nothing to lose and everything to gain by trusting you. Loving Father, I believe you for GREATER as I throw myself at your feet. I will be changed. I will be whole. I will be free and I'll forever praise you. Thank you, Lord. Amen.

Go Deeper

Set aside some time for fasting and prayer over the next week. Let your focus be on the following:

-WORSHIP! Take some time to just worship at the feet of your King. Enjoy pouring your heart out before him. See yourself broken before him and allow his love to minister back to you.

-Facing your shame head on. Ask the Lord to visit each place of shame and mend that place.

-What FREEDOM will feel like for you. Pray in what freedom will mean in your life (e.g. you will no longer hide from a particular person or situation, you'll be able to walk into a new opportunity, etc.). Write down what you see or consider doing a vision board. Keep this handy as a memorial to what God has done in your life.

Selah ~ *Pause, Calmly Think of This*

(The Place of Reflection)

> "You are my hiding place; You preserve me from trouble; You surround me with songs of deliverance. Selah."
>
> Psalm 32:7, NKJV

Oh, beloved one, what a journey! Let's take a moment to Selah. I want you to shut out all of the noise and just think about how far you've come.

Today, be assured of your place in me. We have journeyed together over many miles and we will walk many more. Can you see the footprints of our journey as you ponder how far we've come? I know this road was perhaps not always an easy one to traverse. It called for you to dig deep for strength as you allowed me into places long hidden from the world's view. I saw the places of hurt, shame and defeat that to you seemed insurmountable. Yet you pressed on. Can I just tell you how proud of you I am, lovely one?

So after choosing to walk with me on this journey, beloved, where is your heart in this season? Can we reflect on what this journey has accomplished in you? I desire this to not be a fleeting moment in your life. I want what we've experienced together to be a lasting testament forever. Pivotal moments in life are sometimes best understood in the moments of quiet reflection. Let's take a step back and reflect on our wonderful journey.

Come Away (The Beautiful Invitation)

We began with my beckoning you to come on a journey with me. Remember? You didn't know where we were going, and you initially were a bit hesitant. You were heavy with your yesterday and unsure about your tomorrow. However, you trusted me and my heart leapt for joy.

I asked you first to reflect on my love for you. Having taken this journey now, how has your view of my love changed? Write your reflection here:

I then assured you of my great love for you and how beautiful you were to me ("A lily among thorns"), but we had to deal with barriers to you coming to me. You had a chance to write down those obstacles. What do you think of them now? Are they still there? To what extent? Write your reflection here:

Next, I wanted you to know how much I long to be close to you so I can reveal my heart to you. Remember, I talked about how precious my time was with Adam in the garden. I told you that just as Adam was the apple of my eye, so were you. He knew my voice and I knew just where he was. We were just that close. I said that was my desire – to be that close with you. I wanted you to become more familiar with my character and not just know me by your mere knowledge alone. I asked you what your thoughts were on intimacy with me. Think, my beloved. What are your thoughts now? Write your reflection here:

You also had the chance to go deeper after this chapter. Did you take some time to shut out all voices that are contrary to my voice? Did you develop a game plan on how to deal with the enemy when he attempts to keep you separated from me? How is your game plan working? Write your reflection here:

The Secret Place (The Place of Revealing)

Beloved, then we journeyed to the Secret Place where my desire was to reveal the secrets of my whole heart to you. I knew that this journey to joy had to include a full disclosure of all that I hold in my heart for you. I felt your trepidation but knew that if you could position yourself in the Secret Place and hear from me, it would open up so much in your life. I exposed how the enemy had been working overtime to keep you from hearing from me but I assured you that under the shadow of my wings, you were safe from his withering attacks. You had some thoughts back then on what the Secret Place meant to you. Go back and take a look. Now what do you think? Write your reflection here:

I also spoke to you about enduring the trouble that the enemy created around you: worry, doubt and other nuisances sent to torment you. Facing the enemy alone and uncovered is a horrible predicament to be in. That's why I offered you shelter in the Secret Place. I told you that trouble was an intimidating factor in your life. It rises up to overtake you like a tsunami. Soon you're so disoriented that you don't know how to even move forward. Yet I promised you that I would reveal the schemes of the enemy. I asked you to think about the troubles you were carrying. What of those troubles now? Write your reflection here:

Ah... the intimacy of revelation in the tabernacle, the Secret Place, the place to know me fully and be fully known. It's a vulnerable place, but I tried to comfort your heart by assuring you that you had nothing to hide before me. I reminded you that I see you through the blood of my beloved Son, Jesus. You didn't have to worry about rejection because my arms were wide open before you. I told you that the revelation you would receive from me would allow you to hit the bullseye on the assignments I had for your life and that together, we would redeem the time. I asked you about incomplete assignments in your life. Looking back now, have you begun to work on any of them? Write your reflection here:

You also had the chance to go deeper with prayer and fasting. You were asked to focus on an open, ready and willing heart to accept all that I would reveal to you in this time. I asked you to focus your attention on how you could silence the voice of the enemy. Did you shut him up? Write your reflection here:

The Alabaster Box (The Place of Breaking)

My beloved, then we arrived at the Place of Breaking. I offered you a wonderful opportunity to bring me your alabaster box, full of the worship and tears of a broken past, and break it before me. This baggage was certainly weighing you down, but I knew that getting you to a place of letting it go would be a most difficult thing.

I hoped that the story of the woman with the alabaster box would inspire you. This woman was so beloved by me. When I found her, she was broken. Yet she put her trust in me and found radical deliverance by drawing close to me. Her lavishing such great love on me right before the time of my crucifixion was an act that still rings out throughout time. Oh, what a moment.

I asked you what you thought of this dynamic woman with the alabaster box. Having gone through the breaking of your own box, what do you think of her now? Write your reflection here:

Letting go is tough, my love, and allowing yourself to be broken is no easy decision. I tried to let you know how beautiful your breaking was to me – a complete contradiction to how the world sees brokenness. I knew your first inclination was to hold on tight to the things that have grown so familiar to you even though they hurt you. Could I be trusted to return to you more than you would give up? In the end, we had to confront head on those things you felt like you couldn't let go of. You wrote them down. What of those things now? Were you able to let them go, or are you still holding onto some of them? Write your reflection here:

Next, I promised that your breaking would not result in shame. I assured you that I would honor your great sacrifice. I told you that unlike the brokenness you had experienced in the world, THIS Place of Breaking was much different because instead of a heart all torn apart, you would emerge from this place more beautiful than ever before, more alive than ever before and more TOGETHER than ever before! You could finally be free of the depression, anger, hurt and hopelessness that the enemy would fill your broken places with; and instead, delight in the beauty of a redeemed life – bejeweled in bright colors of deliverance. Oh, I couldn't wait for you to dance with such great joy! I asked you for your final thoughts on the alabaster box (the Place of Breaking). No doubt you had lots of mixed emotions back then. What does your heart say now? Write your reflection here:

In your chance to go deeper, I wanted you to take some time to worship me like the woman with the alabaster box. I also wanted you to face your shame head on and ask me to visit each place of shame and mend that place. Lastly, I wanted you to imagine what freedom would feel like for you. What does freedom feel like now? Write your reflection here:

Conclusion: We covered a lot of ground on this Joyfull Journey. I pray that as you looked back over this wonderful journey, your heart was encouraged. Walking with you has overjoyed my heart, dear one. I'm excited for these next steps with you. Let's go!

Closing prayer: Lord Jesus, this was indeed an amazing journey. Some of the places you led me to were quite hard, but you were right – in every place, I found great joy. I desire more and more to release myself to you. This has been such a good start, but my heart yearns for more. I'm determined that I can't stop now. I don't EVER want our Joyfull Journey to end! Lord, continue to hold me tightly as I go deeper in your truths. I still have some work to do, but I trust you, Great Shepherd, more than ever before. I willingly follow you wherever you lead me with a loving and grateful heart. Amen.

Go Deeper

Set aside some time for fasting and prayer over the next week. Let your focus be on the following:

-Thanking God for all of the work the two of you have done so far. He's worthy of HIGH Praise! Give it to him!

-Continuing to trust him to complete the work. If during your reflection you realized that there was more work to do, take note of those things and press into the Father for answers and strategies. Be like Jacob (Genesis 32:26) and don't let go until he blesses you!

Still Waters

(The Place of Peace)

> "He makes me to lie down in green pastures; He leads me beside the still waters. He restores my soul..."
>
> Psalm 23:2-3, NKJV

Finally, my dear one, I wrap you in my PEACE. Let me seal your Joyfull Journey with a confident assurance that you have come a long way. Though the waters may have been a bit turbulent for a while, never forget that I am the Good Shepherd. I'm faithful. I always lead my sheep to a place of peace.

Today my beloved, you can rest in the fact that you are in a NEW place, verdant and rich. We have been on such an amazing journey – it's o.k. to lie down in the green pastures of my peace right now. The greenness around you signals new life, and with this new vitality comes new strength. Breathe in the free air of this green pasture. Every breath you take in fills you with renewed hope and crazy joy. Take a deep breath now. Can you feel your hope returning?

As a good shepherd, I know my sheep too well. I make it my business to know you better than you know yourself. You see, natural sheep will not drink from a troubled brook. They will only drink and refresh themselves when the waters are calm, so that is where a good shepherd leads them - to still waters. You are the same, my dear child. The troubled water in your life had you very unsettled, so I'm doing the same thing with you. I am leading you to the still waters so that you can be refreshed for the rest of this great journey. The waters here are calm and clear. Drink deeply and allow your soul to be restored.

Tell me...

What does this restoration feel like? Write it here:

> "Peace I leave with you; My peace I give to you; not as the world gives do I give to you. Do not let your heart be troubled, nor let it be fearful."
>
> John 14:27

Wow! My PEACE looks good on you! What I give to you is the REAL DEAL, my love: REAL PEACE... DEEP PEACE. The world offers a counterfeit peace that is fleeting. It satisfies for a while and then, POOF! It's gone, and you're right back to feeling void and empty. You've known this place before but it's not true this time! For this time beloved, you've encountered the only true and lasting peace: Me. Doesn't my Word call me the "Prince of Peace" (Isaiah 9:6).

You no longer have to worry if this peace is going to last. What we've done together is an eternal work. The only way for you to LOSE your peace is for you to RELINQUISH it. I will never take it away. Make sure you never lay it down.

In the coming days, months and years, the enemy will come and try to snatch your peace from you. The inherit evil that is present in the world today certainly has the capability to wear on you and rob you of your peace. But you need only to reflect on all of what we encountered on our Joyfull Journey. My Word says in Psalm 77:6 (KJV), "I call to remembrance my song in the night: I commune with mine own heart: and my spirit made diligent search." You only have to hearken back to the wonderful songs we sang together as we traversed this pathway to peace. When confronted with hellish news, let your heart search and remember the path we took. It will always lead you back to the place of peace.

No more do you have to walk in fear. Your heart can know my assured peace whenever it gets troubled. Know, my love, that I hold your very heart in the palm of my hand and I breathe on every heartbeat. Do you not know that your very heartbeat matches mine? You are not alone. I hold your heart. Remember, you have a great future ahead! Rest in this finished work. Oh, yes, my PEACE looks good on you!

Tell me...

What do you remember most about this Joyfull Journey? Write it here:

Conclusion: Now my beloved, I leave you with a song for those times when you are confronted with dis-ease. May it warm your heart and bring your thoughts right back to me. Be well, my beloved child.

"It is Well With My Soul" ~ Horatio G. Spafford

When peace, like a river, attendeth my way,

When sorrows like sea billows roll;

Whatever my lot, Thou hast taught me to say,

It is well, it is well with my soul.

Refrain:

It is well with my soul,

It is well, it is well with my soul.

Though Satan should buffet, though trials should come,

Let this blest assurance control,

That Christ hath regarded my helpless estate,

And hath shed His own blood for my soul.

My sin—oh, the bliss of this glorious thought!—

My sin, not in part but the whole,

Is nailed to the cross, and I bear it no more,

Praise the Lord, praise the Lord, O my soul!

For me, be it Christ, be it Christ hence to live:

If Jordan above me shall roll,

No pang shall be mine, for in death as in life

Thou wilt whisper Thy peace to my soul.

But, Lord, 'tis for Thee, for Thy coming we wait,

The sky, not the grave, is our goal;

Oh, trump of the angel! Oh, voice of the Lord!

Blessed hope, blessed rest of my soul!

And Lord, haste the day when the faith shall be sight,

The clouds be rolled back as a scroll;

The trump shall resound, and the Lord shall descend,

Even so, it is well with my soul.

www.ingramcontent.com/pod-product-compliance
Lightning Source LLC
Chambersburg PA
CBHW071803040426
42446CB00012B/2683